Cheap and Easy
COOKING

The Survival Guide for College Students

THE CHEF?

Revised Edition
Joe Dobrowolski

S.K.I. Publishing Company

This book is dedicated to my Dad for giving me the motivation to start finishing this book.

Special thanks to Mom, Jenny, Wolfie, Volker, Tony, CC, Jen, Bethany, Aaron and Mr. Yeltsin for the support and advice they provided.
And, of course, Ray and Akbar; thanks for the *Cooking JAR*.

Cheap and Easy Cooking: The Survival Guide for College Students
Published by S.K.I. Publishing Co.

First Printing 1995; "The College Handbook of Cheap and Easy Cooking"
Revised Edition August 1996

Library of Congress Catalog Card Number: 94-12045
ISBN 0-9654612-0-3

Published in the United States of America

Printed in the United States of America

10	9	8	7	6	5	4	3	2	1

Contents

Introduction

I decided to write this cookbook because I couldn't get job after college...
Just kidding. The truth is, I had lots of trouble when I first started cooking
on my own. As a college student, I shared an apartment away from home
for the first time. I had no clue how to cook a decent meal. It was the first
time I was without my parents' delicious meals or even that yummy dorm
food. I had to learn everything from scratch. For a long time I barely sur-
vived on Mac'N'Cheese, cereal, bread and water. Not much of a diet, ehh?

During my days at college, I eventually picked up the hints and tips I
needed to become a proficent *Cheap and Easy* chef. I learned by watching
friends, listening to other peoples ideas and recipes, watching my room-
mates cook and begging them for food, and by trial and error. So I was on
my way to making quick, easy, tasty, cheap meals that would fill me up, and
were easy to cleanup. But why didn't I just read a cookbook?

When I was trying to cook, I wanted a cookbook that had easy-to-follow,
straight-to-the-point directions for quick and simple food. All of the cook-
books that I looked at had obscure recipes that focused on presentation
instead of consumption. The instructions were for elegantly prepared food,
they assumed you knew how to cook and the food always took too long to
make. I didn't want recipes ready to present to royalty. I wanted good
tasting, cheap, filling and hopefully healthy food.

So, armed with my experience, I decided to design this cookbook to follow
these guidelines: concise directions, minimal preparation time, and painless
cleanup. I also added some helpful hints and tips. Then I threw in some
extra thoughts and ideas about food and cooking while trying to keep it
fun. This is what *Cheap and Easy Cooking* is all about!

Keep in mind that I'm trying to take the agony out of cooking, give you
some creative alternative meals and keep you from spending all of your
money on tasty, but expensive pizza and greasy burgers. Enjoy these
delicious meals and any new recipes you devise. Remember to have fun
with all of the time and money you save by using this cookbook.

Shopping Hints

Before going shopping, *try* to plan about 1-2 weeks worth of meals-make a list and check it twice! If you're going to have "Meat Lover's Pasta" (p.35) you should stock up on pasta, and buy some ground beef and sausage and put them in the freezer. Even if you don't know exactly what you are going to eat, buy some items in advance. Just get items like pasta, sauce, rice, meat, frozen veggies and chili in bulk and buy the small stuff and perish- ables, like cream cheese and milk at your local store. It is unlikely that you will have the freezer space or cupboard space to really bulk up anyway.

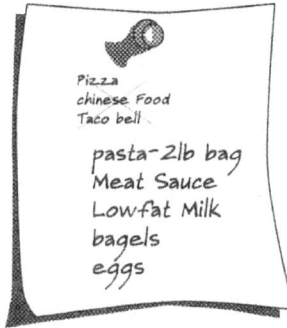

Whenever possible; do as much food shopping as you can at warehouse stores like Price Club/Costco™. Even stores like Pac'N'Save™ are cheaper than local grocery stores.

So buy in bulk when you can. If you're not the commitment type, then don't buy 37 lbs. of baby back ribs. Your best way to save money shopping is to get your parents or relatives to take you and then get them to pay.

How To Read A Recipe*

Chicken Tips

- Boneless skinless chicken breast: Tastes great, quick and easy, but higher in price. If possible, get bulk breast.

- Use any substitute piece of chicken instead of chicken breast if you prefer. Skin and bone as needed.

- Sauté (a fancy word for fry) chicken in a pan: *Add 1/2 cup of water to help the frying.* Don't add water to hot oil!

Tips: pointer to be aware of for general preparation

Approximate cooking time and cost

Dish/Meal title

Basic Baked Chicken   22 Min $2.75

Special info — *Yields 4 servings*

Ingredients —
I or 2 Chicken breasts
I Egg
1/2 Cup milk
1/2 Cup flour

Optional Ingredients —
(Italian seasonings, paprika, dash of salt)

1. Preheat oven to 350°
2. Beat egg and milk together.
3. Mix flour, *seasonings* in a bag.
4. Dip each piece of chicken in egg/milk mix, then shake inside bag.
5. Bake chicken for 15-20 minutes in a baking dish (metal deep dish pan).

Detailed cooking Instructions

Specific hints and tips

*See page 30
**See page 18
***See Chicken on Rice™

* Yes, you would have figured out how to read a recipe without this handy helper, but keep in mind that I wanted to make the cooking as painless as possible. This could help you...... and it looks really cool.

Things To Remember

1. The ingredients in *italics* are always optional, but that does not mean that the non-italicized ingredients are always essential. In this example, the chicken is obviously essential. In other recipes, I list the items that I prefer to use. The optional ingredients represent what I or other people do when there is extra time. I urge you to experiment like crazy.

2. Before starting a recipe, read the general and specific hints. Give the directions a once over, then start cooking.

3. The cost and cooking time will vary depending upon the equipment, ingredients, and stores. I gave the best possible estimate for each meal.

4. Microwave cooking times vary based on the oven size and wattage.

5. When I refer to a "med-high pan," it is intended that you preheat the pan to this temperature as well as cook at this temperature.

6. Don't get discouraged if your food isn't perfect the first time. Try, try again. You will get better in the kitchen and your meals will begin to taste absolutely fantastic and soon you will become a master *Cheap and Easy* Chef!

In the Kitchen

First you need to get some kitchenware. There are two ways to do this: buy it or have someone give it to you. Beg your family and friends for some donations, then go to thrift stores and garage sales to get the rest.

Blender: Great to have around. $15-40+ new. $1-20 used.

Colander: Just a Holy bowl for draining water from pasta.

Cutting - Knives: Buy a used, small, *sharp*, solid knife ($5.^{00}) or get the fabulous new Ginsue II for an amazing price, just $19.^{95}-Act Now!

Cutting Board: Along with your knife, buy a small cutting board (about $1.^{00} at garage sales). Look for the plastic type.

Extras: Three best bets: Olive oil, garlic, fresh basil.

Oil: Regular cooking oil is cheap and can be substituted for olive oil in any recipe, but olive oil adds flavor to the food.

Oven: Usually bake at 350°- 375°. When baking, the oven is up to temperature when the little red light turns off. When broiling, turn dial to broil, get coils red hot, insert food, and leave door slightly open.

Microwave: Get a large and small microwave dish, both with lids, they can double as storage containers. Ceramic dishes can be used in the micro or on the stove. (NO metal or aluminum foil in the microwave, unless you want to see lightning!)

Measuring: This is the difference between great and bad meals. Yeah right, maybe with French cuisine. It's more important to have a general idea of measurements. For example: a 'cup' of water is about the same as 4 full shot glasses, a 'dash' is more than a pinch, but less than a pour, a 'teaspoon' is less than a 'tablespoon' which is about the size of a big spoon.

Pan/Pots: Get 1 large pot, 1 small sauce pan and 1 frying pan, each with a good cooking surface.

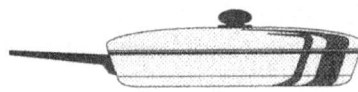

Storage: Keep ample supplies of aluminum foil and Ziploc® bags. Have at least 1 large and 1 small Tupperware™ container.

Seasonings: Individual seasonings are great by pricey. Mrs. Dash™ and Pappy's Choice™ are ready-made mixes of seasonings in one bottle. They are easy to use for lots of recipes and they're quick, *cheap and easy*; just like the book title said it should be.

Breakfast

Simplest & Cheapest Meal®   1 Min $0.00

Your roommate's cereal
Someone's milk and butter

1. Pour cereal and milk in a bowl.
2. Toast bread; butter to taste.

Not So Boring Cereal Mix #1   1 Min $0.80

I Serving kix®
I/2 Serving cocoa puffs®
Milk

1. Combine the two cereals for extra flavor; add milk.
2. Drink the chocolate milk for a complete breakfast.

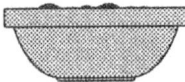

Not So Boring Cereal Mix #2   1 Min $0.75

I Serving rice krispies®
I/2 Serving fruity pebbles®
Milk

1. Combine cereals.
2. Pour milk.
3. Eat.

Healthy Not So Boring Cereal Mix   1.2 Min $0.70

I/2 Serving wheaties®
I/2 Serving total®
I/2 Serving frosted flakes®
Milk

Combining these cereals gives 100% of the RDA nutrition for 15 essential vitamins and minerals as well as needed beta carotene, but it also tastes good and has a bit of sugar to jump-start your day. Add juice, toast, 3 spoonfuls of sugar, and a pot of coffee to get you completely wired and ready for class.

French Toast the Easy Way®   2.8 Min $0.40

2 Slices frozen french toast   1. Toast the slices.
Butter   2. Butter each slice.
Syrup   3. Pour syrup and enjoy.

French Toast the Hard Way   10 Min $0.75

3 Eggs   1. Combine milk, *rum* & eggs in a
I Cup milk   bowl and whip up.
Butter   2. Add some cinnamon & sugar.
4-6 Slices of bread*   3. Pour mixture into a bowl large
Syrup   enough to fit a piece of bread.
Cinnamon   3. Soak both sides of each slice in the
(Powdered sugar)   mixture until soft, but not soggy.
(Strawberries)   4. Sauté each slice on a buttered pan
(I Tablespoon rum)   at med-high until slightly brown
                                         on each side, and the middle isn't
                                         soggy.
                                      5. Serve with syrup, butter, strawber-
                                         ries, powdered sugar, or other.
                                      *Wierd, but hard bread doesn't get as
                                      soggy in mixture, so leave the bread out
                                      over night to get hard.

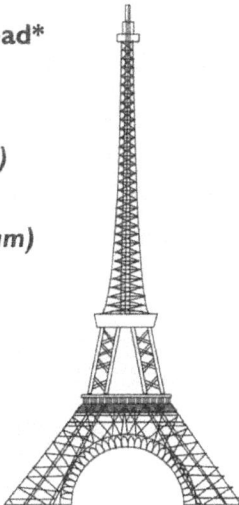

Waffles the Easy Way®   3 Min $0.50

3 Frozen waffles   1. Toast waffles.
Butter   2. Butter the middle slice.
Syrup   3. Cover with syrup.
                                      4. Microwave for 20 sec.
                                      5. Eat while hot.

Pancakes

10 Min $1.50

Yields 5-6 Pancakes

Pancake mix
1 Egg
1/2 Cup milk
2 Teaspoon oil
(Butter)
(Syrup)

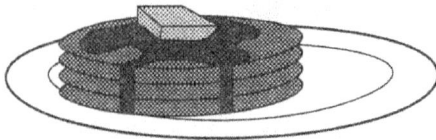

1. Mix the first four ingredients together until smooth.
2. Heat a large pan or griddle to med/med-high.
3. In the pan pour a 4 inch circle of batter for each pancake.
4. Flip when little bubbles cover top, and bottom is golden brown, about 1 min.

Heat pan or griddle until a drop of water will move around, but will not disappear right away (toooo hot!) or flatten out and sizzle (toooo cooool).

Less milk for thicker pancakes.

Speedy Morning Muffin

2 Min $0.20

1 Muffin
2 Slices cheese

A. Toast muffin, then melt cheese on muffin in micro.
B. Melt cheese on muffin in toaster oven for 45 sec.

Cream Cheese Bagel

2.4 Min $0.48

1 Bagel, any style
1 Knifeload cream cheese

1. Cut bagel in half.
2. Toast bagel.
3. Spread cream cheese.
4. Eat and Run. Yahoo!

New

AM Big Ben   2 Min $0.30

2 Split english muffins
4 Slices deli meat i.e. ham
2 Slices cheese

Toaster oven:
> Place cheese on one slice and meat on the other. Toast for 1.5 min on low. Put together and chow.

Microwave:
> Toast muffin in a conventional toaster. Place cheese on meat, cook in micro for 30-40 sec.

Breakfast Shake   4 Min $0.32

2 Scoops vanilla ice cream
I Egg white
1/2 Cup O.J.
1/2 Cup milk
(1/2 Banana)
(Yogurt-any flavor)

1. Put all ingredients into an electric blender.
2. Blend until smooth.
3. Adjust amount of O.J. and milk to suit taste.
4. (Add the *banana* to make it tasty and healthy).

Substitute the ice cream with lowfat or nonfat yogurt for a healthy twist.

Bacon   3 Min $0.25

2 Strips of Bacon
[2 Paper towels]

Micro:
> Put a paper towel on a plate. Lay bacon on the towel, cover bacon with 2nd towel. Cook for 45 sec per piece.

Frying pan:
> Lay bacon strips in a med-heat pan. Cook for about 2 min or until desired browness is reached. Flip bacon after 1 min.

Sunny-Side Up Eggs   4 Min $0.25

2 Eggs

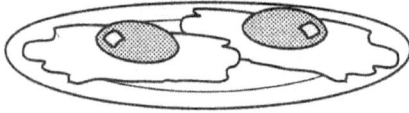

1. Crack both eggs into a med-heat frying pan. Be careful not to break the yolk (yellow).
2. Fry until the white is firm.

   Without a non-stick pan, add a teaspoon of butter or some Pam® to the pan

Yummy Scrambled Eggs™   6 Min $0.69

It's healthy because of the "egg whites," but the cheese and meat make it yummy.

2 Eggs
2 Egg whites
Cheese
I Turkey slice

1. Crack 2 eggs into a cup.
2. Use only the whites of the other 2 eggs. Crack egg, then pour out the white without breaking or spilling the yolk (yellow).
3. Whip up the eggs into a frothy frenzy with a fork.
4. Next grate a bit of cheese and chop the meat.
5. Combine ingredients.
6. Pour mixture into a med-high frying pan and scramble with a spatula to desired taste.

The Egg: Exposed

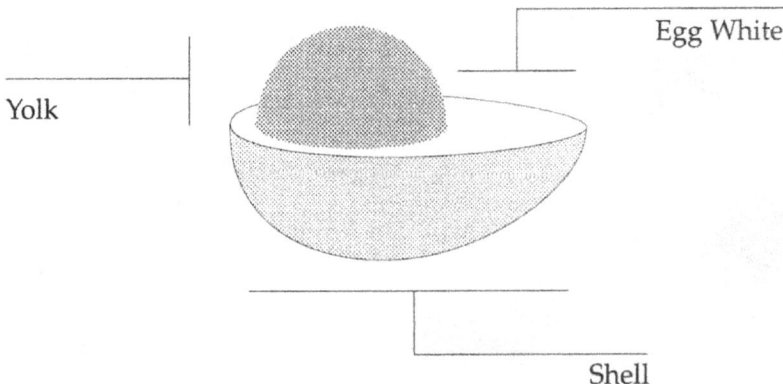

Egg White

Yolk

Shell

Microwave Scrambled Eggs   3 Min $0.45

4 Eggs

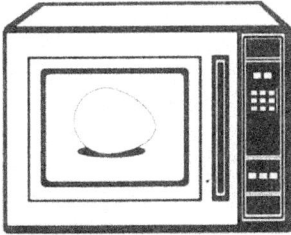

1. Crack eggs into a bowl*.
2. Whip eggs.
3. Cook the eggs on high for 45 sec per egg (2:40 for 4 eggs).
4. Stir eggs well.
5. Then microwave for another 10 sec per egg.
6. Stir and eat.

*A large bowl is quite appropriate.

Scrambled Eggs   4 Min $0.51

4 Eggs

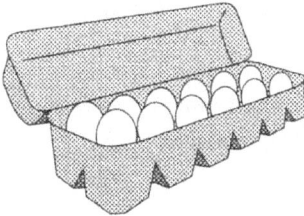

1. Crack eggs into a bowl.
2. Whip eggs.
3. Pour mixture into a med-high frying pan.
4. Using a spatula, stir and flip the eggs around until they are as browned or as runny as you desire.

Over Easy Eggs   4 Min $0.25

2 Eggs

1. Crack both eggs into a med heat frying pan. Be careful not to break the yolk (yellow).
2. Fry until the white is firm.
3. Flip each egg "over easy" with a spatula and fry for 20-30 sec more.

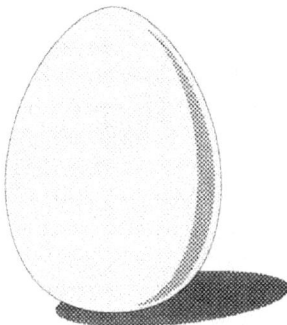

Ranchero Omelette · 7 Min · $0.99

3 Eggs
Splash of milk or water
2 Tablespoons butter
2 Tablespoons salsa
Small cube of jack cheese
(Cooked shrimp or ham)
(Salt and pepper)

1. Whip eggs, milk, *seasonings*.
2. Pour into a med-high buttered pan.
3. Reduce heat to med, allowing eggs to cook until moist & firm.
4. Add salsa and cheese.
5. Optional items should be warmed before added.
6. Fold omelet in half with a spatula.
7. Top it with more salsa

Breakfast Quesadilla · 5 Min · $0.35

1 or 2 Eggs
1 Slice cheese
1 Tortilla
(Sausage)

1. Scramble the eggs*.
2. Fry sausage for 2-4 min until browned in same pan.
3. Melt cheese on tortilla in micro or toaster oven.
4. Chop sausage into pieces.
5. Combine and eat.
   *see page 16

Eggs MacMuffin · 5 Min · $0.45

1 Egg
1 English muffin
1 Slice of cheese
(Bacon or ham)

1. Toast muffins.
2. Cook egg* sunny-side up or scrambled.
3. Fry *bacon*** with the egg.
4. Melt cheese onto muffin in microwave or toaster oven.
5. Combine and eat.
   *see page 16
   **see page 14

Lunch

Guac Dip   7.2 Min $1.31

Yields 6 servings

Ripe avocado

2 Tomatoes*

I Small green (long) onion*

I Fresh hot green chili pepper*

(Salt)

(Chips)

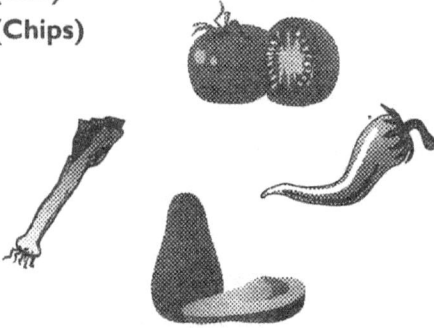

1. Peel avocado, pit, then mash with a fork.
2. Dice tomatoes (better if skinned, not necessary).
3. Finely chop the onion and chili pepper.
4. Combine all ingredients in a bowl and mix.
5. Serve at once with chips.

   *Salsa can be substituted for these if you are lazy... uh, I mean, if you have no time.

   Adding 1/2 teaspoon of lemon keeps extra guac from turning brown.

The Big Melon Salad   6 Min $Var

Best served when fruit is in season; spring and summertime.

I/2 Cantaloupe

2 Slices watermelon

I/2 Honeydew

1. Peel, core, pit and slice fruit.
2. Toss in a bowl and serve.

Energy Shake, Shake, Shake   2.1 Min $0.70

Great after a workout. Easy, nutritious and tastier than A Pound of Hangover Cure.

I/2 Cup flavored lowfat yogurt

2 Egg whites*

I Banana, peeled

I Teaspoon sugar

1. Throw everything into a blender.
2. Blend until smooth.
3. Drink up.

   *Substitute with an egg substitute mixture substitute as a substitution.

A Pound of Hangover Cure   4.5 Min $1.25

First run half a mile, drink this shake with a few asprin, shower, find an ice pack, then zzzz...

1 Egg white
1/2 Carrot
1 Teaspoon peanut butter
1 Teaspoon (*nonfat*) yogurt
1/2 Cup prune juice
1/2 Cup tomato juice

1. Blend all ingredients until smooth.
2. Grin and bear it.

Fruit Freezie   2.999999 Min $1.11

1 Cup milk
6 Crushed ice cubes
3/4 Cup diced fresh fruit*
(*1 Egg*)
(*1 Tablespoon honey*)

1. To crush the ice, place the milk and ice into the blender and let it grind.
2. Add fruit, *honey* and egg; blend for about 30 sec.

*Apples, strawberries, peaches, apricots, pears, cantaloupe, and/or watermelon.

Lunch in a Glass   5.07 Min $0.89

1 Banana
1 Apple (without core)
1 Peach (without pit)
1/2 to 3/4 Cup orange juice
20 Raisins

1. Slice up the fruit.
2. Blend all ingredients until smooth.
   Do not try to use a straw with this one?!?!

Random
Graphic

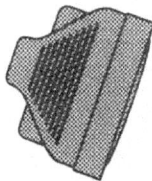

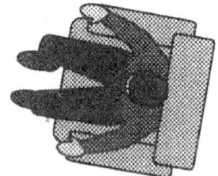

Micro-Melt Quesadilla   3 Min $0.15

3 Slices jack cheese
I Tortilla

1. Grate cheese onto tortilla.
2. Roll cheese inside tortilla.
3. Micro for 45 sec.

Original Quesadillas   4 Min $0.20

3 Slices jack cheese
I Tortilla
Bit o' butter

1. Melt butter in a frying pan at med-high heat.
2. Place tortilla in pan.
3. Grate cheese onto tortilla.
4. Fold tortilla in half, fry both sides until golden brown.
5. Cut into 4 pieces and eat.

Mexican Style Quesadilla   6 Min $1.05

Yields 3 Quesadillas
3 Tortillas
4 Slices jack cheese
I/2 Can (8 oz) refried beans
Pat of butter
(Salsa, hot or mild)

1. Combine grated cheese and beans in a pot.
2. Heat at med-high for 2 min, until bubbly.
3. Place tortilla in a buttered frying pan, then scoop mix onto it.
4. Fold in half and fry until golden brown.
5. *Add salsa.*

Mexico   The World

Super Quesadilla   9 Min $3.09

Yields 4-6 Quesadillas

1 Can refried beans
6 Leaves iceberg lettuce
2 Tomatoes; red & firm
Small block of jack cheese
4-6 Tortillas
(Sour cream, guacamole, salsa)

1. Put beans in a bowl and micro-wave on high for 1.5 min.
2. Dice tomatoes, shred lettuce, and grate cheese into separate bowls.
3. Place slices of cheese on the tortilla and microwavefor 30 secs.
4. Place the tortilla and cheese in a buttered frying pan...then...
5. Put the first 4 ingredients in the frying tortilla.
5. Fold in half and fry until the tortilla is golden brown.
6. *Add salsa, guacamole and sour cream.*

Tuna Mix   3 Min $1.00

2-3 Cans tuna in spring water
2 Spoonfuls of mayonnaise

1. Drain the water from 2 or 3 small cans of tuna.
2. Mix up the tuna and mayo in a Tupperware™ container. Store it, ready to go, in fridge.

Tuna Sandwich   2 Min $0.40

Tuna mix
2 Slices of bread
(Mustard)

1. Spread the tuna *and mustard* on the bread.
2. Eat up.

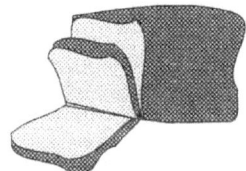

Tasty Tuna Melt   4 Min $0.60

Tuna mix
2 Slices of bread*
Cheese
Mustard

1. Place cheese over tuna mix on a slice of bread.
3. Spread mustard on the bread.
2. Toaster oven for about 1.5 min; or microwave for 45 sec.
4. Eat up.

*Microwaving cheese on bread works best if the bread is toasted first to avoid soggy bread!

Pizza Sandwich   8.1 Min $0.60

I Roll
Pasta sauce
Mozzarella cheese
(Sausage, pepperoni, ham)

1. Spread pasta sauce on one half of the roll.
2. Cover sauce with grated cheese *and sliced meat.*
3. Place open roll in oven.
4. Bake for 3-5 min @ 350° or toaster oven it at low for 3-5 min.

PIZZA

Hey, Let's make some pizza sandwiches for lunch.

The Mini-Sub   4 Min $0.85

I Sesame seed roll
2 Pieces mild cheddar cheese
2 Slices honey turkey*
2 Slices ham*
Mayo
Mustard

1. Open roll.
2. Micro cheese on roll bottom at high for 40 sec.
3 Spread mayo and mustard on roll top conservatively.
4. Place turkey and ham over the melted cheese.
5. Close the roll.
6. Toast in toaster oven for 1.5 min @ light until the bun is golden brown.

*Substitute any type of deli meat.

Fire Two!

Quickie Meat Melt   5 Min $0.35

This sandwich works best with a toaster oven, or oven.

4 Pieces of deli meat
2 Slices of bread
2 Slices cheese
(Tomato)
(Lettuce)
(Mayo)
(Mustard)

Toaster oven:
Layer deli meat and cheese slices between the bread. Place in oven until cheese has slightly melted (about 1.5 min).

Microwave:
Toast one slice of bread. Spread cheese on this slice. Micro slice for 20-35 sec, add deli meat slices, slap on the other slice of bread and munch away.

Get creative with *tomato, lettuce, etc.* (time permitting, of course.)

Grilled Cheese   4 Min $0.60

2 Slices of bread
2 Thin slices mild cheddar
  cheese
2 Thin slices of jack cheese
Dollop of butter

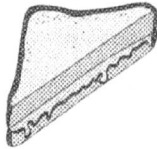

1. Warm a small frying pan to med-high.
2. Butter 2 slices of bread, place butter side down in pan.
3. Place cheddar on 1 slice of bread and jack cheese on the other.
4. Fry bread until golden brown.

   Simple style: Microwave cheese on toasted bread fo 45 seconds.

Sloppy Potato   35 Min $1.07

This is a great one pot meal with minimal cleanup.

I Can chili
2 Potatoes

1. Bake 2 potatoes in oven at 350° for 25-35 min.
2. Empty can of chili into a pot. On the stove, warm the chili at med-low until bubbling, then set heat to low until potatoes are done baking.
9. Break open top of potatoes, mash the inside and filli with chili.

   Faster version: 13 min $1.05
   Microwave 2 potatoes for 10 min at high.
   Microwave chili for 1.5 min at high.

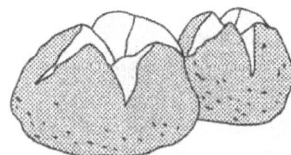

Dinner

Frozen Veggies-Stove Top   8 Min $0.75

Yields 2 large servings

1/2 Bag frozen mixed veggies
1/4 Cup water
(Pepper)

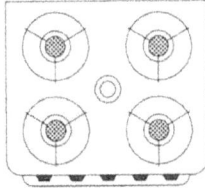

1. Boil water in a pot.
2. Pour veggies into pot.
3. Stir and bring to a boil again (about 2 min).
4. Cover, reduce heat to low.
5. Done when veggies are tender (about 5-7 min).
6. Season and serve.

Frozen Veggies-Microwave   8 Min $0.72

Yields 2 large servings

1/2 Bag frozen mixed veggies
1/4 Cup water
(Pepper)

1. Place veggies in a microwaveable dish.
2. Add 1/4 cup of water.
3. Cover and cook on high for about 5-7 min.
4. Stir once during cooking.
6. Season to taste and serve.

Dad's Mashed Potatoes   20 Min $0.76

3 Large potatoes or
  4-5 small potatoes
1/4 Cube butter
1/4 Cup milk
(1 Spoonful of sour cream)
(Pepper)
(Salt)

1. Peel the potatoes and dice into medium-sized pieces.
2. Boil potato pieces until soft: Try 15 min then test with a fork to see if it's soft.
3. Chop butter.
4. Combine ingredients and beat*.

*For fluffiest results, use an electric beater.

Garden in the Salad   10 Min $1.75

Yields 5-8 servings (a weeks worth).

**6-18 Leaves iceberg lettuce, red-
leaf lettuce, and/or spinich***

2 Tomatoes, red & firm

I Cucumber

1/2 Avocado

(Sprouts)

(Salad dressing-ranch)

1. Shred lettuce.
2. Dice tomatoes.
3. Peel cucumber, slice and dice it.
4. Cut avocado in half, twist it, then leave pit inside other half, remove skin and dice avacado half.
5. Combine all and toss it up.
6. Serve with *dressing*.

*Store uneaten salad in Tupperware™. Place paper towels on top of the salad, close lid, then place it upside down in the fridge so it will stay fresh longer.

Line the bottom of your crisper with paper towels, then you don't have to leave the veggies in plastic bags. You need to check the crisper at least every two weeks for spoiled food. Change the paper towels every 2 months or more.

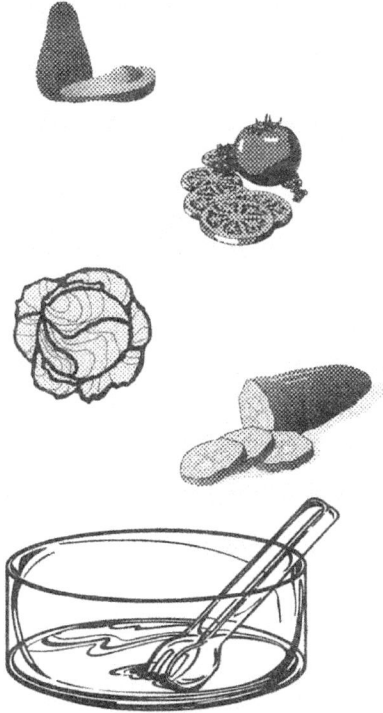

1008
Island
Ranch
Dressing

Express Salad   4 Min $1.25

Yields 3-4 servings (a weeks worth.)

**1/2 Bag fresh express salad
mix™-American style**

I Tomato

(Salad dressing-any style)

1. Open salad mix*.
2. Dice tomato.
3. Combine salad mix and tomato.
4. Serve with *dressing*.

*Keep remaining salad fresh. Store it in the bag, tied with a rubber band.

Camping Chili   10 Min $3.25

This is called camping chili because it is a one pot meal, which is especially useful when camping. Also when sharing a sink with other people. Yields 4-6 servings

I Can meat chili

I Small can kidney beans

I Small can tomato paste

I Can kernel corn

1/2 Cup grated cheese

I Small can diced olives

Tortilla chips

(Salsa)

1. Drain water from corn.
2. Combine chili, beans, tomato sauce, corn, salsa and cheese in a large pot.
3. Cook at med-high for 6-7 min, stirring occasionally until bubbly.
4. When warm, add 2 handfuls of crushed chips, or put the chips on top, uncrushed.

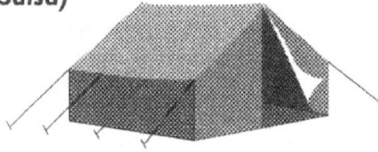

For cheaper and easier Camping Chili, add cheese, salsa, chips to canned meat and bean chili.

Dan Q. Boiled PotatoE   1 Min $0.19

I Med potatoE

(I Teaspoon salt)

(Scoop of butter)

Dog
Patotoe
Presedint

1. Add enough water to cover potatoE in a big pot.
2. Add 1 teaspoon salt.
3. Cook in rapidly boiling water until tender, about 15-25* min.
4. Break potatoE top and *add butter*.

*Depending on size of potatoE

Microwave Rice   30 Min $0.24

Yields 2-4 Servings

I Cup rice

2 1/8 Cups water

(Seasonings)

1. Combine 1 cup of rice and 2 1/8 cups of water in a microwaveable container.
2. *Add a bit of pepper and salt.*
3. Microwave for 7.5 min on high and 7.5 min on power level 4 (i.e. a less than 1/2 power).
4. Let rice hang out for 15 min.

Top O' The Stove Rice   25 Min $0.43

Yields 3-5 Servings

1 Cup rice

2 Cups water

(1 Teaspoon salt)

(Dollop of butter)

1. Boil 2 cups of water (*add butter and salt*) in a large pot.
2. Stir in 1 cup of rice.
3. Cover pot, simmer at low until rice is tender and water is absorbed; about 15-20 min.
4. Let stand for 5-10 min.

10 Minute Rice, Rice Baby   12 Min $0.31

Cook this one as if you were cooking pasta.

1 Cup rice

2 Cups water

Pat of butter

(1 Teaspoon of salt)

(Other seasonings)

1. Boil 2 cups of water in a large pot.
2. Add 1 cup of rice to the rapidly boiling water.
3. After 10 minutes, drain using the lid.
4. Add butter, salt and other seasonings and stir once or twice to avoid a sticky spot on the bottom of the pot.

Quick and Nice Minute Rice   11 Min $0.29

1 Cup "minute" rice

1 Cup water

(Seasonings)

(Tid bit of butter)

1. Start boiling the water.
2. *Add pepper, salt and butter to the water.*
3. Put the rice into a cup.
4. When water is boiling, pour rice into pot, stir briefly, quickly cover the pot, then remove from heat.
4. Wait 10 minutes, then it's done.

Minute rice usually comes in a box.

American Burrito   12 Min $3.25

Yields 4-6 Burritos

6 Leaves iceberg lettuce
2 Tomatoes, red & firm
1/2 Lb beef or chicken
Small block of jack cheese
4-6 Tortillas
(Sour cream)
(Guacamole)
(Salsa)

1a. Cook ground beef or chicken in a med-high frying pan until brown.
1b. Chop chicken into small chunks. In a med-high frying pan, sauté chunks for 4-5 min in a thin layer of oil and water.
2. Dice tomatoes, shred lettuce, and grate cheese into separate bowls.
3. Warm tortillas in microwave
4. Scoop desired amount of each item into tortilla, add salsa, guacamole and sour cream, fold and eat.

Save the extras in the fridge and warm up for a quick meal or snack.

Sloppy JOE Burrito   10 Min $2.75

Yields 6 burritos

1/2 Lb beef or chicken
Small block of jack cheese
1/2 Cup salsa, hot or mild
4 Oz tomato sauce
Tortillas
(8 Oz refried beans)
(Salt and pepper)

1. Cook ground beef in a med-high frying pan until brown.
2. Grate cheese.
3. Mix all ingredients in pot.
4. Heat on med-high until bubbly (2 min).
5. Scoop desired amount of mix item into tortillas. Fold & eat!

The Art of Burrito Folding

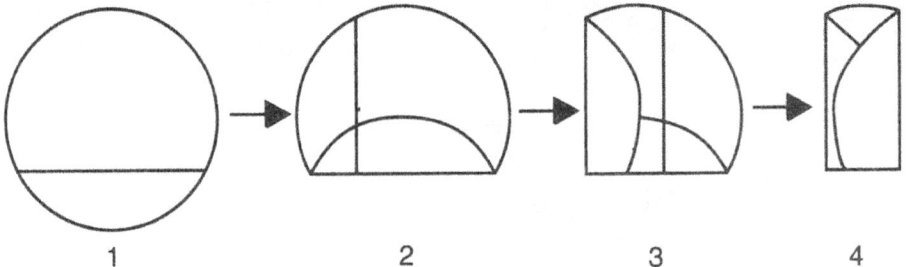

1   2   3   4

- You can never have too much pasta. It's cheap, easy, and great for you. You will soon discover that **pasta is** *Cheap and Easy Cooking!*

- Everyone knows spaghetti, but there are many other types of pasta out there, such as egg noodles, rigatoni, angel hair, vermicelli, rotelle, elbow, fettuccini, and more.

- Buy the sauce mixes in the seasonings aisle; they're easy and tasty.

- After bringing water to a boil, reduce heat to med or med-low, it will cook the same and will save a little $$$$$$$. Remember to stir.

- Putting oil (in the boiling water) keeps the noodles from sticking together and helps keep the water from boiling over.

- Wash the noodles after cooking them by running them under hot water for a few seconds.

- Al dente means that the noodles are slightly under-cooked. Some people prefer this style.

- Buy the largest bag of pasta and jar of pasta sauce, thus you can cook enough for leftovers.

Pasta Hints and Tips

Spaghetti   10 Min $1.25

1/2 Bag of spaghetti
12 Oz sauce
Water
(1 Teaspoon oil)
(Mrs. dash or mr. pappy's)
(Parmesan cheese)

1. Bring half a pot of water and oil to a boil.
2. Add spaghetti to boiling water.
3. Boil at med for 6-8 min. Stir occasionally.
4. At the same time warm the sauce in another pot at low.
5. Drain pasta in a colander.
6. Scoop sauce onto a plateful of spaghetti. *Add cheese.*

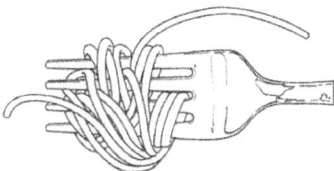

Try various store bought bottled sauces, like Ragu®.

1 Pot Pasta   10 Min $1.75

Another college staple meal you should get to know.

3 Cups of elbow noodles
12-15 Oz ragu® meat sauce
Water
(1 teaspoon of oil)
(Parmesean Cheese)

1. Bring half a pot of water *and oil* to a boil.
2. Add noodles and boil at med-high for 6-8 min.
3. Drain pasta in a colander.
4. Warm sauce in the empty pot, then add the noodles.
5. Sprinkle on parmesean cheese.
6. Stir and serve.

Rockin' Ramen   6 Min $0.25

This is the #1 all-time starving student cheapo meal plan.

Ramen style noodles
Pasta sauce
(Seasonings)

1. Cook ramen noodles in boiling water for 4 min.
2. Strain noodles with pot lid.
3. Add sauce to noodles in the pot.
4. Set on med for 2 min and stir.
5. Add noodles and seasonings for a good cheapo meal.

Mac 'N' Cheese   10 Min $0.75

This is a simple college staple one pot meal. I have even resorted to using water instead of milk and butter. The epitome of cheap and lazy, I mean...easy.

1 Box mac 'n' cheese
1/4 Cup milk
1/2 Cube butter
1 Tablespoon oil

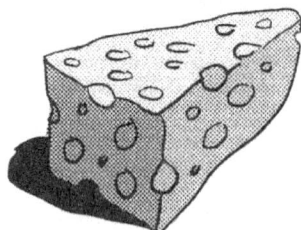

1. Bring water and oil to a boil.
2. Add noodles, cook for 7 min, stirring often.
3. Melt cube of butter over low heat.
4. Add strained noodles to buttery pot.
5. Over low heat, stir in milk and flavor packet .

Meat Lover's Pasta   9 Min $2.25

1/2 Bag egg noodles
1/2 Jar meat flavored sauce
1/4 Lb ground beef
1 or 2 Chopped sausages

1. Cook noodles for 5-7 min.
2. Fry beef and sausage in a med-high frying pan at for 6-8 min, then pour off fat.
3. Strain noodles.
4. Combine sauce, meat and noodles in the pot and warm for 1 min.
5. Scoop, serve and eat.

Angel Hair Primavera   11 Min $2.55

1/4 Bag angel hair pasta
Primavera sauce
Milk
Butter
Oil

1. Boil water and oil.
2. Cook pasta 4-6 min.
3. Warm primavera sauce over low heat.
4. Dish out sauce conservatively over angel hair pasta, and serve.

Primavera sauce is in the pasta section of the store.

Chicken Fettuccini Alfredo   11 Min $3.50

1/4 Lb chicken
1/2 Bag fettuccini
1 Bag alfredo sauce mix
3/4 Milk
1/3 Cube butter
Oil

Mr. Al Fredo

1. Boil water and oil.
2. Cook pasta for 8 min.
3. Bone/skin/chop chicken.
4. Sauté chicken pieces for 3-4 min in a thin layer of oil and water.
5. Prepare Alfredo sauce: Over low heat, stir milk and sauce mix into a pan of melted butter. Bring to a boil, then reduce heat to med-low, cook for 5 min.
6. Add chicken to sauce then scoop onto the pasta.

Double Bacon Cheeseburger   8 Min $2.70

Yields 2 Burgers

3/4 Lb ground beef
2 Buns
2 Slices jack cheese
2 Slices bacon
(Mayonnaise)
(Lettuce)
(Tomato)
(Mustard)

1. Knead 2 balls of meat into flat hamburger patties.
2. Cook patties in a med-high frying pan for 3 min per side.
3. Microwave bacon or cook next to the patties*.
4. Toast bun bottom of buns in the toaster or on the frying pan.
5. Melt cheese onto buns in the microwave (20-35 sec).
74. *Spread mayo and mustard onto the bun tops.*
91. Combine and eat.
    *see page 15

Outdoor Pizza Burgers   13.2 Min $2.65

Yields 2 Burgers

3/4 Lb ground beef
I Dash parmesan cheese
1/4 Can diced olives
(I Dash oregano, crushed)
I Dash pepper
2 Oz Tomato sauce
4 Slices mozzarella cheese
I Tomato sliced
2 Buns, split & toasted

0. Prepare coals.
1. Combine meat and next 5 items and knead in to balls.
2. Smash balls into flat patties, slightly larger than the bun.
3. BBQ both patties over med-high coals for 7 min.
4. Flip each patty, then top with cheese and tomato.
5. BBQ for 4 more min.

Burgers On the Grill   8 Min $1.95

Yields 2 Burgers

3/4 Lb ground beef
BBQ sauce
2 Buns
(Seasonings)

1. Mix seasonings and BBQ sauce into 2 balls of meat.
2. Smash balls into flat patties, slightly larger than the bun.
3. Cook for about 3 min on each side, depending on thickness.

- Firing up the BBQ: Put the charcoal in a pyramid in the center of the coal rack, use lighter fluid and let burn for 15+ min.

- Finding the right BBQ temp: Hold hand at cooking height over burning coals. Count how long you can hold your hand there. 2 seconds = very hot, too hot. 3 seconds = med-high/hot. 4 seconds = medium. 5 seconds = low.

- For more heat, tap ash from coals and push the coals closer together. For less heat spread out the coals.

- Let the grill top heat up, then grease it with trimmings.

- Trim outer edges of fat so drippings won't flame up.

- With a fatty patty, put the meat around the outside of the grill.

- Quench flames by sprinkling the flames with water.

- When broiling and grilling, cook 1st side longer than 2nd

- Seasonings: Don't salt uncooked meat. Pepper and salt the browned meat right after turning.

- BBQ cooking times don't include coal preparation.

BBQ Tips

The Grilling Guide

Food	Coal Temp	Cook Time	Other Info
Hamburger	Hot	Side 1: 5 min = med-rare 6 min = med Side 2: 4 min	
Tender Steak: *Sirloin,* *Porterhouse*	Hot	Side 1: 7 min = med-rare 9 min = med Side 2: 6 min	1/2 inch thick steak.
Other Steak: *Chuck, Cube,* *Flank*	Med	Side 1: 9 min = med-rare 12 min = med Side 2: 8 min	Marinate for hours. Baste while cooking. 1/2 inch thick steak.
Shrimp	Hot	5 min	Turn once.
Pork Chops	Hot	5-6 min per side	
Chicken	Med-Hot	4-6 min per side	Thin Breast or Wings.
Corn on Cob	Hot	10-20 min	In foil, season and butter.
Sausage (Precooked): *Franks,* *Keilbasa*	Med-Low	5-15 min	Depending on size.

Shrimp on the Barbie   10 Min $2.93

1/3 Lb raw shrimp
4 Cracker, crushed
1 Egg, slightly beaten
1 Teaspoon olive oil
(Sprinkle of parm cheese)

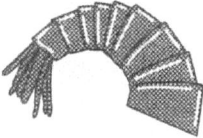

0. Prepare coals (hot).
1. Let stand in oil for 1 min.
2. Dip each shrimp in egg, then in cracker/cheese crumbs.
3. Broil over hot coals for 5-8 min, until crumbs are browned.
4. Skewer or put shrimp on foil to prevent falling through the grill.

Corn on the Cob on the Que   23 Min $0.31

Some ears of corn
Margarine or butter
Salt and pepper

0. Prepare coals (hot).
1. Husk each corn.
2. Cover corn with butter and seasonings.
3. Wrap aluminum foil securely around each ear of corn, but don't seal the sides.
4. Cook on hot coals for 15-20 min.
5. Turn frequently.

BBQ (Garlic) Minute Steak   6 Min $2.91

2 "Minute steaks"
Butter
Aluminum foil
(Garlic)

0. Prepare coals (hot).
1. Make a foil pan, big enough for the steaks by turning up the edges of the foil.
2. Melt *garlic* & butter in foil pan.
3. Place minute steaks in pan, on top of grill.
4. Cook over hot coals for 2-3 min per side.

It is easier than you think to do steak right. It just takes a few tries to get a feel for it. Especially considering the various types of steak cuts. Soon you will be making steak perfect every time.

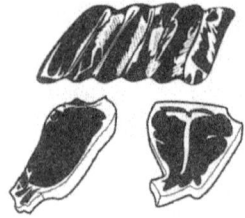

The best and more expensive cuts are: New York, Porterhouse, Eye of Round, Filet Mignon and some others. They are $5+ per lb. The cheaper cuts that taste good are "Top Round, Bottom Round, Rib-Eye, and many more." $3-4 per lb.

To get a juicier steak, it is best to marinate it before cooking. Favorites include beer and red wine, as well as BBQ sauce, or a mix of oils and sauces. My favorite is Worcestershire sauce. Partially fill a Ziploc® bag with your chosen sauce. Insert meat and let it sit in the fridge for 2 or more hours. If time is short, put the meat in a thin layer of sauce for 5-15 minutes while preparing the rest of the meal.

Seasonings (such as garlic, sweet basil, Mrs. Dash™/ Mr.Pappy's™ and pepper) are another key to creating a tastier steak. Use any kind you want. Before cooking, sprinkle seasonings on both sides of meat for added flavor.

Some people prefer sautéed onions, garlic and mushrooms. To sauté, fry chopped garlic, onions and/or mushrooms in *olive* oil for 8-10 minutes at med-heat. Then top the finished steak.

Another cow tip: Never try to tip over a sleeping cow. Remember what happened to Chris Farley in *Tommy Boy*? Besides, it would be a little emabarrassing to explain the criminal charges to a future employer....."Uh, well it was sleeping, I just kinda, you know, pushed it."

Broiled Steak   10 Min $4.50

See the steak section to the left, you can't miss it.

1/2 Inch thick steak

(Seasonings)

(Marinating items)

(Garlic)

(Onions)

(Mushrooms)

1. Marinate steak.
2. Set oven to BROIL.
3. Cover a pan with aluminum foil (for easier cleanup).
4. Place meat on pan.
5. Pour the juices from the package onto the steak before placingthe steak in the oven.
6. Put the steak on the top oven rack (close to the heat).
7. Cook for 3 min* on the first side, then flip.
8. After 3 min on side two, take the steak out and cut the middle to check pinkness. If it's not done**, put in for another minute, but don't flip it, leave it on the second side for the rest of the broiling. Continue until the steak is done.
9. *Serve with sautéed garlic, onions and mushrooms.*

*Depending on the thickness (not overall size) of the cut. For thin cuts it may only take 2 min, while thick cuts can take up to 6 min a side.

**Here, done refers to "medium-rare," meaning slightly pink in the middle. You should cook it more or less depending how much you want it to Moo!

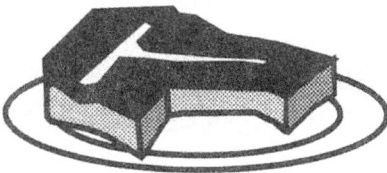

If you are considering going out to a nice dinner, reconsider! Make it yourself. It's a great way to impress your special lady friend, favorite man or some friends, and it's really not that hard. You can turn an OK meal into *fine dining* just by adding wine and bread.

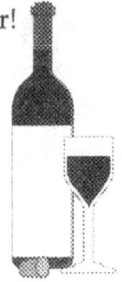

Although fine dining is oxymoronic here, let me tell you how it 's done the *Cheap and Easy* way. If you make two or three dishes, and serve wine, it becomes a more elegant meal. You are adding flair to the presentation. Also adding a loaf of bread creates the image of a "complete" meal, yet it is *cheap and easy* to prepare! Either serve a loaf of bread with butter on the side, or split a loaf, lightly cover it with garlic and butter and toast in the oven. You can cook both the meat and bread in the oven together; just remember to take the bread out.

Here is a fine example: Prepare steaks, veggies and rice served with Sauvignon Blanc. Another choice would be angel hair primavera, baked and battered pork chops, garlic bread and White Zinfandel. Or choose my famous chicken fettuccini alfredo, an express salad, french loaf and Johannesburg Riesling. These are complete meals and will take a little longer than any individual dish in this cookbook, but think about the attention and respect you will earn. Not to mention that your guests will have to treat you next time.

But you say, "how do I choose the correct wine for each meal." Check out the wine hints on the next page. Now you are set for a great dinner. Enjoy!

Choosing wine is easier than you thought. All wines priced less than $10-12 are fairly equal in quality (excluding night train, thunderbird, screw-tops and the likes). You can get a good wine for $4-5! Choose wines that go with most meals. Most people enjoy sweeter, smooth, mellow wines. It's hard to go wrong with these wines: A red (looks pink) called White Zinfandel; whites: Sauvignon Blanc or Johannesburg Riesling.

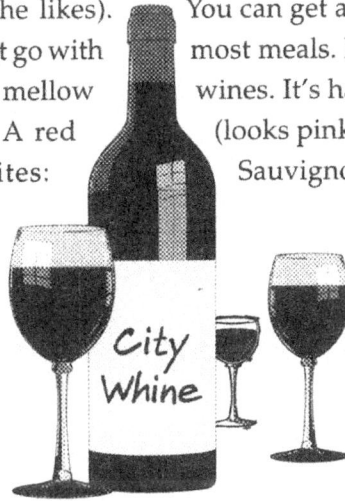

City Whine

Never buy or order the San Francisco wine. This does not mean Napa, just San Francisco. If you do try out this flavor, you will be served with: "It's too foggy in San Francisco, it's too expensive, there are too many hills, the clubs aren't open late enough, there are never any cabs, there is too much traffic, there are....."

White wines should always be drunk as soon as possible, as they do not age well. Red wines, on the other hand tend to get even better with age. White wines shoud be refrigerated. Red wines can be left out to help them age.

Wine Tips

Chicken Tips

- Boneless skinless chicken breast: Tastes great, quick and easy, but higher in price. If possible, get bulk breast.

- Use any substitute piece of chicken instead of chicken breast if you prefer. Skin and bone as needed.

- Sauté chicken in a pan. *Add 1/2 cup of water to help the frying.* Don't add water to hot oil!

Honeyed Chicken   15 Min $2.15

Fancy! Yields 4 servings

2 or 3 Chicken breasts
1/2 Cup honey
Olive oil
Bread crumbs
Parsley, thyme, basil, pepper

1. Dip each piece of chicken in enough honey to give a thin coat.
2. Mix enough crumbs and seasonings to fill 1 cup.
3. Coat honeyed chicken with crumb mix.
4. Heat a thin layer of oil in a med-low frying pan.
5. Arrange pieces in a single layer, cover and cook for 10 min. Flip a few times.

Chicken Fried Rice   22 Min $2.75

Like Chicken'N'Rice™. But everything is thrown in together and fried. Yields 4 servings.

1 or 2 Chicken breasts
1 Cup rice
2 Cups frozen mixed veggies
2 eggs
Olive oil
(Italian, garlic, pepper)
(White wine)
(Teriyaki sauce)
(Soy sauce)

1. Start rice.*
2. Scramble 2 eggs.**
3. Sauté chopped chicken.***
4. Throw all ingredients into a large pan or wok, set to med-low.
5. Add seasonings and teriyaki sauce or soy sauce. Stir it around for about 2 min, or until brown.

*See page 30
**See page 17
***See Chicken'N'Rice™

Chicken 'N' Rice   25 Min $2.25

This chicken dish is a nutritious and filling meal. Try it!

I or 2 Chicken breasts
I Cup rice
Olive oil
(Italian, garlic, pepper)
(White wine)
(Teriyaki sauce)

1. Start the rice*
2. Chop up the chicken breasts.
3. Prepare the pan: Add enough oil *(add white wine or teriyaki sauce for better taste)* to cover the bottom then heat to med-high.
4. Toss chicken into the pan and *add seasonings.*
5. Cook the chicken: Sauté for 2-4 min, until the center is no longer pink, stir and flip each piece 2 or 3 times.
6. Mix the chicken and the rice in a bowl and eat. Add Teriyaki sauce.

*See page 30

Basic Baked Chicken   24 Min $2.75

Yields 4 servings.

I or 2 Chicken breasts
I Egg
1/2 Cup milk
1/2 Cup flour
(Italian seasonings, paprika, dash of salt)
[Paper bag]

1. Preheat oven to 350°.
2. Beat egg and milk together.
3. Mix flour, *seasonings* in a bag.
4. Dip each piece of chicken in egg/ milk mix, then shake inside bag.
5. Throw chicken into a baking dish (metal deep dish pan).
6. Put chicken in the oven and bake for 15-20 min.

Broiled Mustard Pork Chops   10 Min $2.25

2 Pork chops
Mustard-any style
(Seasonings)

1. Set oven to BROIL.
2. Spread mustard and *seasonings* on both sides of each pork chop.
3. Place on broiling pan or foil.
4. Broil for 4 min on first side.
5. Flip, broil 3-4 min until done.

Baked, Beaten and Battered Chops   15 Min $2.25

2 Pork chops
Bread crumbs*
I Egg
Milk
(Parmesan cheese)
(Italian seasoning)

1. Set oven to 375°.
2. Mix egg and an equal amount of milk in a bowl.
3. Spread bread crumbs, *parmesan cheese and seasonings* on a plate.
4. For each chop, dip both sides into egg mix then lay each side on the crumbs.
5. Place chops on foil or in a pan for 8-12 min.

*These can be bought or made by crushing stale bread.

Can't Elope Tonite   3 Min $1.00

I Ripe cantaloupe
2 Scoops ice cream
Squirts of whip cream

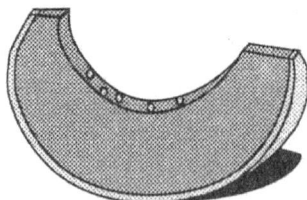

1. Cut cantaloupe in half.
2. Remove seeds.
3. Now fill the hole with ice cream.
4. Add whip cream on top.

About the Author

Joe Dobrowolski is a graduate of the University of California at Davis. While there he studied Managerial Economics. This is his first cookbook and it seems to have little, if anything, to do with his studies of management economics. Joe is currently cooking up these recipes and many more in San Francisco where he resides. And he still talks about himself in the third person.

www.ingramcontent.com/pod-product-compliance
Lightning Source LLC
Chambersburg PA
CBHW071745020426
42331CB00008B/2179